THE DEBT IN AMERICA

An overview of consumer's debt, household loan and its impact on u.s citizens

JAMES D JOHN

Disclaimer

This book is intended for informational purposes only. The information contained herein is based on the author's research, analysis, and interpretation of available data at the time of publication. While every effort has been made to ensure the accuracy of the content, the author, publisher, and any associated entities make no guarantees about the accuracy, completeness, or suitability of the information for any particular purpose.

Contents

Introduction

In the United States, the economy is a constant balancing act of dreams and demands. For many, it's a story of hopes for a better life, often entangled with financial pressures that come with debt—be it from a home, an education, or even day-to-day living expenses. At nearly $18 trillion, American household debt stands at a record high, a massive figure that could overwhelm even the wealthiest of nations. But there's a paradox: while debt has soared, so too have incomes, and despite mounting IOUs, many Americans are managing to stay afloat. Yet, for millions of households, the line between stability and financial stress is razor-thin, a delicate equilibrium shaped by shifting wages, inflation, and interest rates.

This book, Debt vs. Income: The American Financial Balancing Act, unpacks the intricacies of this economic paradox. It explores not only the numbers but the human lives behind them. We dive into the forces driving household debt upward and the ways disposable income is rising to keep pace. We'll delve into what these trends mean—not only for our collective economic health but for individuals, families, and future generations trying to make sense of the American dream in today's financial landscape.

At the heart of this analysis lies a vital question: Are Americans managing debt sustainably, or is this precarious balance masking an underlying crisis? This book addresses that question by examining the latest data, assessing the policies shaping our economic environment, and offering insights into the tools households can use to navigate the future. Alongside the detailed examination of interest rates, income trends, and inflation, we also explore practical paths toward financial resilience—actions individuals can take to shield themselves from economic shocks and thrive, regardless of the broader financial weather.

As you turn the pages, expect to find not only figures and forecasts but stories and strategies. Debt vs. Income is both a guide to understanding the economic landscape and a toolkit for building personal financial security in an uncertain world. This is the American financial balancing act, and it's one that affects us all. Welcome to a deeper understanding of debt, income, and the pursuit of stability in the modern American economy.

Chapter 1:

A Snapshot of American Debt - Understanding the Growing Figures

The United States has reached an unprecedented level of household debt. As of the third quarter of 2024, American household debt reached a record $17.94 trillion, underscoring both the accessibility and dependence on credit and loans for millions of Americans. This chapter explores the structure of household debt in America, delves into the driving forces behind its growth, and provides historical context to understand its significance.

Overview of American Household Debt

Household debt in America comprises several key categories: credit cards, auto loans, mortgages, and student loans. Each of these categories reflects different aspects of American financial behavior, consumer needs, and economic realities. The Federal Reserve Bank's Quarterly Report on Household Debt and Credit is the primary source of detailed data on these figures, offering insights into trends, risks, and economic behaviors tied to debt accumulation.

Credit Card Debt:

Credit card debt is often regarded as one of the most concerning categories due to its high-interest nature and its use for everyday expenses. As of recent figures, credit card balances have seen substantial increases, as inflation continues to impact household budgets. For many Americans, credit cards act as a buffer against rising costs, even though this type of debt can become unmanageable if not controlled. Credit card debt has been steadily increasing as consumer spending remains robust, despite inflationary pressures and elevated interest rates.

Auto Loans:

Another major category is auto loans, which have been climbing steadily due to both rising car prices and growing demand. The pandemic-era supply chain disruptions led to a shortage of both new and used cars, pushing prices to historic highs. This, combined with low financing rates early in the pandemic, led to a boom in car purchases. Today, auto loans have continued to rise as Americans rely on personal vehicles, and prices for new and used cars remain high.

Mortgages:

Mortgage debt is traditionally the largest component of household debt in the U.S. Due to the importance of homeownership in American culture, many households carry mortgage debt as a necessary part of achieving the American dream. Historically low interest rates spurred homebuying in recent years, leading to higher mortgage debt. With home prices remaining elevated, mortgages continue to represent a significant portion of overall household debt.

Student Loans:

Student loan debt remains a critical and often debated category of American household debt. While it hasn't grown as dramatically in recent years, it is still a substantial burden for millions of Americans. Student loans affect younger generations disproportionately, often delaying homeownership, family planning, and other financial milestones.

Role of the Federal Reserve Bank's Quarterly Report on Household Debt and Credit

The Federal Reserve Bank's Quarterly Report on Household Debt and Credit serves as a key resource for tracking U.S. debt patterns. This report compiles and analyzes data on household debt balances, delinquency rates, and trends across different debt categories. The information helps policymakers, economists, and the public understand shifts in economic behavior and assess financial stability.

For instance, when debt increases are observed across categories like credit cards and auto loans, the report helps identify broader economic factors, such as inflation or changes in consumer spending habits. It also tracks delinquency rates, providing a view into potential risks for financial institutions and the economy. Understanding debt trends is essential for assessing the economic well-being of American households and for making informed policy decisions aimed at safeguarding financial stability.

Factors Driving Debt Growth

The increase in household debt in the U.S. can be attributed to a combination of demographic, economic, and social factors. Here, we examine several key drivers: population growth, the rise of online shopping, increasing vehicle costs, and high inflation.

Population Growth and Urbanization:

Population growth naturally contributes to the rise in household debt, as more people means more households taking on debt for homes, vehicles, education, and daily expenses. Additionally, the trend toward urbanization places greater financial pressures on households. In cities where the cost of living is high, many people rely on credit to maintain a certain quality of life or cover unexpected costs.

The Rise of Online Shopping and Consumer Spending:

The shift to online shopping has also influenced debt growth. With the convenience of e-commerce and access to a wider range of goods and services, consumers are spending more than ever before. Many of these purchases are made using credit, particularly credit cards, which can quickly lead to debt accumulation. The ease of online transactions, coupled with targeted advertising, has contributed to an increase in spending behaviors that, in turn, drive up debt levels.

Increasing Vehicle Costs:

The price of cars, both new and used, has soared in recent years. Supply chain disruptions caused by the COVID-19 pandemic created shortages, leading to higher prices. As car ownership is a necessity for most Americans, especially those outside of major cities, people have been willing to take on more debt to secure vehicles. Even as supply chains have stabilized, the elevated prices have not significantly decreased, and auto loans continue to be a significant source of debt for American households.

High Inflation and Economic Pressures:

Inflation has been a critical factor in driving up debt. The U.S. has faced decades-high inflation rates recently, which impacts nearly every aspect of household budgets, from groceries to utility bills. In response to these rising costs, many Americans have turned to credit to cover everyday expenses. Inflation also affects long-term purchases, as the cost of financing a home or a car increases with rising interest rates.

Economic Context

To fully understand the current debt levels, it is helpful to place them in historical context. Comparing today's figures with past debt levels reveals patterns that reflect broader economic cycles, such as recessions and periods of economic growth.

The 2008 Financial Crisis:

The financial crisis of 2008 was a turning point in American debt history. During this period, household debt reached a peak debt-to-income ratio of 120%. Much of this was due to the mortgage market, where risky lending practices led to widespread mortgage defaults. The crisis triggered a recession that had long-term effects on lending standards, consumer behavior, and the financial system. In response, banks became more cautious about lending, and households were more conservative with credit, at least for a time.

Pre-Pandemic Debt Levels (2019):

By 2019, before the COVID-19 pandemic, the debt-to-income ratio had dropped to 86%, reflecting a period of economic stability and recovery from the Great Recession. Unemployment was low, and wages were growing at a steady pace, allowing many households to manage their debt levels more effectively. Mortgage debt remained the largest category, but credit card and auto loan debts were also prominent as consumer confidence was high and interest rates were relatively low.

Pandemic and Post-Pandemic Debt Trends:

The COVID-19 pandemic led to a unique economic environment. To stimulate the economy and support households, interest rates were slashed to historic lows, leading to a boom in borrowing, especially in the housing market. Many Americans refinanced mortgages or bought new homes at record-low rates, which temporarily boosted household debt. Government stimulus checks also helped some households pay down debt, but others used credit to weather economic uncertainty. As the economy recovered, inflation surged, leading to higher interest rates, which has since influenced debt growth in the auto loan and credit card sectors as well.

In 2024, the current debt-to-income ratio of 82% signals that household debt, while high, is relatively manageable compared to previous economic cycles. Nonetheless, the elevated levels across various categories demonstrate a reliance on credit to maintain standards of living in the face of rising costs. This balance between manageable debt levels and the risk of economic stress due to inflation and high-interest rates continues to define the financial landscape for American households.

Chapter 2:

Debt vs. Income

The American Financial Balancing Act dives into the income perspective as a potential counterbalance to rising debt levels among Americans. This chapter examines recent income growth trends, the role of employment and wage increases in sustaining household financial health, and the disparities in income distribution that affect economic stability across demographics and sectors.

Income Growth Overview

Disposable personal income in the United States has reached a significant milestone, now totaling $21.8 trillion. This figure represents not just the overall income growth in the economy but also hints at American households' resilience in an environment where debt has been steadily rising. One of the most notable aspects of this income growth is its pace compared to debt accumulation, providing a form of economic relief. Recent data reveals that the U.S. debt-to-income ratio currently stands at 82%. This ratio, which reflects the share of disposable income dedicated to repaying debts, has improved considerably from past years; in 2019, it was around 86%, and during the peak of the 2008 financial crisis, it surged to a staggering 120%.

This drop in the debt-to-income ratio highlights a meaningful shift in the financial dynamics of American households, indicating that income growth has outpaced debt increases. Although debt levels continue to rise, driven by factors like inflation, consumer spending, and high living costs, the parallel growth in income helps many households better manage their obligations. For policymakers, economists, and financial experts, this trend underscores the critical importance of income growth as a stabilizing force for the economy. When disposable incomes rise at a faster pace than debt, households generally experience less financial strain, which can lead to healthier spending habits and a more robust overall economy.

Employment and Wage Growth

The role of the labor market in fostering income growth cannot be overstated. The U.S. labor market has shown remarkable resilience, sustaining one of the longest periods of expansion in recent history.

For 18 consecutive months, wage growth has outpaced inflation, signaling a shift in the economic environment. This achievement is crucial because, for a substantial period, inflation had outstripped wage gains, eroding purchasing power and placing strain on household budgets. Now, with wage increases outpacing inflation, many Americans are finding their financial footing once again.

A strong labor market benefits households by providing steady employment, which is essential for income stability. When unemployment rates are low, workers have greater bargaining power, leading to higher wages and better job security. Currently, unemployment levels have remained low, with steady job creation across various industries. This environment fosters confidence among workers, encouraging them to spend and invest in ways that contribute to economic growth. With a robust job market, households can plan for their financial future with more certainty, whether that means saving for emergencies, investing in education, or making large purchases like homes or cars.

The sectors showing particularly strong employment growth include healthcare, technology, and professional services, which typically offer higher wages and opportunities for career advancement. On the other hand, lower-paying sectors, like retail and hospitality, have also experienced growth but often lag in wage increases. However, even these industries have seen some gains, largely due to the competitive hiring market that has put pressure on employers to increase wages to attract and retain workers.

The significance of sustained wage growth cannot be overstated, especially given that it has outpaced inflation consistently for more than a year. This trend translates to real gains in purchasing power for American families, providing them with the flexibility to manage or even reduce their debt. When wages grow faster than inflation, households can meet their basic needs more comfortably and allocate a larger share of their income toward debt repayment, savings, or investments, which helps to strengthen their financial health over the long term.

Income Distribution and Disparities
Despite these positive trends, income growth in the U.S. is far from uniform. Variances in income growth across demographics and economic sectors highlight disparities that continue to shape the financial well-being of American households. Income distribution in the U.S. remains uneven,

with significant gaps between different demographic groups, regions, and industries.

One of the most notable disparities exists along racial and ethnic lines. Studies show that Black and Hispanic households tend to have lower median incomes compared to White and Asian households. This income gap is partly due to historical inequities and limited access to high-paying jobs in certain sectors. For example, while the technology and finance sectors have seen impressive wage growth and employment opportunities, these fields remain less accessible to minorities, who are underrepresented in such high-income fields. Addressing these disparities requires targeted policy interventions and organizational commitments to diversity, equity, and inclusion.

Gender also plays a significant role in income distribution. Women, on average, earn less than men, even in similar roles and sectors. Although the gender pay gap has narrowed over recent decades, it persists, especially in male-dominated industries like technology, finance, and engineering. Moreover, the pandemic exacerbated these issues, as women were disproportionately affected by job losses in service sectors and faced greater caregiving responsibilities, which impacted their ability to participate fully in the labor market. The long-term impact of this imbalance affects income stability and household debt levels, as lower income translates to fewer resources for savings and debt repayment.

Regional disparities further complicate the picture of income distribution in the U.S. In coastal areas like California and New York, incomes tend to be higher due to the concentration of high-paying industries, such as technology, finance, and entertainment. In contrast, states in the Midwest and the South generally have lower average incomes, often because the dominant industries—such as manufacturing and agriculture—pay less. The cost of living also varies widely across regions, with residents in high-cost areas needing higher incomes to maintain the same standard of living as those in lower-cost regions. These regional income disparities affect households' ability to manage debt and achieve financial stability.

Educational attainment remains one of the most powerful predictors of income, with college graduates typically earning significantly more than those without a degree. However, the rising cost of higher education poses its own set of challenges, as many students take on significant debt to fund their studies. While college graduates may earn more over their lifetimes, the debt they incur for their education can delay financial milestones like homeownership and retirement savings. Furthermore, the high costs associated with education limit access for lower-income families, perpetuating income inequality across generations.

Income inequality has broader implications for debt and economic stability. Households with lower incomes are more likely to rely on credit for basic expenses, making them vulnerable to accumulating high-interest debt, such as credit card balances. Without sufficient income to cover rising living costs, these households may fall behind on payments, leading to higher delinquency rates and financial instability. In contrast, higher-income households can often manage debt more effectively, as they have greater financial flexibility and access to lower-interest borrowing options, such as mortgages and student loans.

Addressing income inequality is essential for promoting economic resilience across all demographics. Policy solutions may include raising the minimum wage, expanding access to affordable education, and creating initiatives that promote equal pay across genders and ethnicities. Additionally, programs that provide job training and reskilling opportunities can help workers transition to higher-paying fields, especially as industries evolve and technology advances. These efforts can narrow income disparities and foster a more inclusive economic landscape where all households have the financial means to manage debt sustainably.

Chapter 3:

The Delinquency Dilemma - Balancing Income Growth with Financial Stress

While American incomes are generally rising, the persistent increase in household debt continues to present challenges for many families. Debt delinquencies — instances where borrowers fall behind on their payments — have remained a focal point in understanding the current economic landscape. Despite a strong job market and growth in disposable income, many households still find themselves struggling to meet financial obligations on time. This chapter delves into the complex dynamics driving these delinquency trends, exploring the interplay of income growth, inflation, and regional and demographic factors that contribute to financial stress.

Current Delinquency Trends

According to recent data from the Federal Reserve Bank of New York, delinquency rates have been rising across several major categories of household debt, most notably in credit card and auto loan payments. Credit card balances, in particular, have seen a marked increase, with consumers relying heavily on revolving credit to cover expenses amid high inflation and elevated interest rates. As of the latest report, credit card debt has grown at a historic pace, with delinquencies beginning to tick upward after a period of relatively stable payment behavior during the height of the COVID-19 pandemic.

Auto loans, another significant category, have also seen a surge in both balances and delinquencies. Factors contributing to this rise include the increased cost of vehicles, both new and used, along with higher interest rates, which raise monthly payment requirements. The New York Fed's data points to a concerning trend: despite a generally favorable economic environment, more Americans are falling behind on their car payments, often due to inflationary pressures impacting other essential areas of spending, such as food, housing, and healthcare.

While delinquency trends in mortgage and student loan debt have remained more stable, these categories are not immune to potential challenges. For mortgages, delinquencies have been kept relatively low, partly due to the substantial equity many homeowners have accumulated in their properties. However, with rising interest rates potentially dampening housing market activity, mortgage delinquencies could become a concern if economic conditions shift. Meanwhile, the current pause in federal student loan payments has temporarily masked the true scope of student debt delinquencies. As repayment requirements resume, there is potential for increased stress among borrowers, particularly those whose income gains have not kept pace with the cost of living.

Moderation in Delinquency Trends: A Mixed Picture

Despite the upward trajectory in delinquencies, the data also indicates some moderation in these trends, which the New York Fed characterizes as "cautiously positive." While delinquencies are rising, they are not doing so at the alarming rates seen during past economic downturns, such as the 2008 financial crisis. This moderation may be attributed to several factors. First, the robust job market has provided many households with consistent income streams, even in the face of inflation. Second, wage growth has, for the past 18 months, kept pace with or outstripped inflation, helping households manage debt more effectively than they might have otherwise.

However, the relative moderation in delinquency rates should not overshadow the underlying financial stress many households are experiencing. Elevated prices across essential categories mean that even with income gains, the cost of living is still burdensome for many, leading some households to rely on credit just to make ends meet. For example, the continued pressure of high food, energy, and healthcare costs often leads to a juggling act, where households prioritize immediate needs and defer debt payments as a last resort. This cycle of financial trade-offs reflects the precarious balancing act many households face between income and debt obligations.

Causes of Delinquencies Amidst Rising Income

One of the perplexing aspects of the current economic climate is the persistence of delinquencies even as household incomes rise. A closer analysis reveals several factors contributing to this phenomenon. Chief among them is the impact of inflation, which has eroded the purchasing power of households, despite increases in nominal income. While wages have been growing, they have not always kept pace with inflation's cumulative impact over time, meaning that the real value of income gains is often less than it appears.

High inflation rates have also led to significant cost-of-living adjustments for basic expenses, including rent, groceries, and utilities. For many families, these adjustments have meant that a larger portion of their income is devoted to maintaining current standards of living, leaving less available for debt repayment. This squeeze on disposable income often leads households to prioritize immediate living expenses over debt obligations, resulting in delayed payments and, in many cases, higher delinquency rates.

The impact of rising interest rates cannot be overstated in understanding delinquency trends. The Federal Reserve's monetary policy response to inflation — a series of rate hikes — has directly affected the cost of borrowing. Higher interest rates have made it more expensive to carry balances on variable-rate debt like credit cards, exacerbating financial strain for households already struggling with high prices. Auto loans and new mortgages have also become more costly, as higher interest rates translate to larger monthly payments. This dynamic means that even if incomes are rising, the increased cost of debt servicing can offset the benefits of income growth, creating a situation where delinquencies persist despite higher earnings.

Moreover, delayed payments and rising interest rates can have a compounding effect on financial health. As households fall behind on payments, late fees, and penalty interest rates add to the principal owed, making it even harder to catch up. Over time, this accumulation of debt can lead to credit score declines, reduced access to affordable credit, and, in severe cases, a cycle of financial instability that is difficult to escape.

Regional and Demographic Analysis of Debt Stress

While delinquency trends reveal overarching patterns in household debt, a closer look at regional and demographic data highlights disparities in financial stress across different groups. Geographic and socioeconomic factors play a significant role in shaping household debt experiences, with some areas and populations facing higher rates of delinquencies than others.

From a regional perspective, states with higher living costs tend to report higher delinquency rates. For example, households in cities with elevated housing costs, such as San Francisco, New York City, and Los Angeles, may struggle more with maintaining timely payments due to the significant portion of income devoted to rent or mortgage payments. In contrast, areas with lower living costs may see fewer delinquencies, though this varies depending on local economic conditions and employment opportunities.

Income level is another critical factor in delinquency trends. Lower-income households are more likely to experience financial stress and, consequently, higher delinquency rates. These households typically have less access to credit, fewer savings to buffer against financial shocks, and a larger share of their income dedicated to essential expenses. Even modest increases in the cost of living can push low-income households into delinquency, especially in high-inflation periods when even basic needs become harder to afford. Conversely, higher-income households are often better positioned to absorb economic shifts, given their greater financial flexibility and access to resources.

Age also influences delinquency trends. Younger adults, particularly those in their 20s and 30s, often carry high levels of debt due to student loans, credit cards, and, in some cases, mortgages. This demographic may experience more frequent delinquencies as they juggle these debt obligations with relatively lower income levels early in their careers. Middle-aged adults, typically those in their 40s and 50s, may also experience financial stress, particularly if they are supporting dependents, managing large mortgages, or coping with healthcare costs. However, older adults, particularly those over 65, generally have lower delinquency rates, as many are either retired with fixed income sources or have paid off significant portions of their debt.

In addition to income and age, racial and ethnic disparities in financial health are evident in delinquency data. Minority groups, including Black and Hispanic households, tend to have higher delinquency rates compared to their White and Asian counterparts. This disparity is often linked to longstanding income and wealth gaps, which limit financial stability and access to credit for minority communities. Structural inequalities, such as disparities in educational and employment opportunities, further exacerbate these financial stressors, making debt management more challenging for these groups.

Chapter 4:

The Inflation Effect - Navigating the Dual Pressures of Prices and Payments

Inflation is one of the most pervasive forces in the economy, affecting nearly every aspect of household finances. For American families, rising inflation creates a unique challenge: maintaining purchasing power while managing debt and expenses. This chapter examines how inflation has shaped household debt, affected consumer spending, and led to significant changes in financial behaviors.

Impact of Inflation on Debt and Spending

As inflation rises, so does the cost of goods, services, and financing, affecting household debt levels in several ways. One major area impacted by inflation is auto loans. In recent years, the cost of new and used vehicles has surged due to supply chain constraints, semiconductor shortages, and high consumer demand. Consequently, many households have been forced to take on larger auto loans, with longer repayment terms and higher interest rates. When car prices increase faster than incomes, Americans are often left with little choice but to finance these purchases with debt, increasing their vulnerability to future economic shifts.

Mortgages have also been significantly impacted by inflation. Housing prices have seen sharp increases in many regions, fueled by high demand and limited supply. As a result, potential homeowners are either borrowing larger amounts or being priced out of the market altogether. Higher mortgage balances have long-term implications, particularly in an inflationary environment where interest rates are also rising. For borrowers with adjustable-rate mortgages, the impact can be particularly pronounced, as they may face escalating monthly payments that strain household budgets. Even fixed-rate mortgage holders may struggle as their real purchasing power declines, making it more difficult to meet monthly obligations.

Credit card debt is another area where inflation's effects are acutely felt. When the cost of everyday essentials—groceries, gas, utilities—rises, many households turn to credit cards to bridge the gap between income and expenses. As prices increase, so do the balances on these accounts, compounding financial strain. Credit cards carry some of the highest interest rates of any consumer debt type, meaning that inflation can quickly turn temporary financial fixes into long-term debt challenges. This reliance on credit cards during periods of high inflation can result in a cycle where consumers continuously accrue debt to cover essential spending, ultimately creating a debt trap that's hard to escape.

In sum, inflation amplifies the financial burden on households by making big-ticket purchases and everyday necessities more expensive. This often pushes families to rely on debt to maintain their standard of living. However, as debt balances rise, so do monthly payments, which can lead to further dependency on credit and limited financial flexibility.

Income vs. Inflation Over Time
One of the most critical factors in managing inflation is the rate of income growth. Ideally, income growth should outpace inflation, allowing consumers to retain their purchasing power. However, this has not always been the case. For 25 consecutive months during the recent inflation surge, prices rose faster than incomes, squeezing

household budgets and leading to a drop in real disposable income. This period of inflation outpacing income growth was particularly challenging for lower-income households, which spend a larger proportion of their earnings on necessities like food, housing, and transportation. As these costs rose, many households found themselves in precarious financial positions, forced to cut back on non-essential spending or rely more heavily on credit.

More recently, however, there has been a positive shift. Over the past 18 months, income gains have exceeded inflation, providing some relief for consumers. This improvement can be attributed to several factors, including a strong labor market that has led to wage increases across various sectors. Government stimulus efforts during the pandemic also bolstered savings and purchasing power for many households, helping them manage the impacts of inflation. Additionally, as the Federal Reserve has raised interest rates to curb inflation, the rate of price increases has moderated, allowing incomes to catch up.

The relationship between income and inflation is crucial for household financial stability. When incomes grow faster than inflation, consumers have more flexibility to manage rising prices and are less likely to rely on debt. This creates a virtuous cycle where households can save, invest, and spend without needing to take on additional financial obligations. However, when inflation outpaces income growth, the reverse happens: households become more dependent on credit, have less room for savings, and face increased financial stress. This dynamic underscores the importance of wage growth in maintaining economic stability, especially during periods of inflation.

Consumer Behavior Shifts in an Inflationary Economy

High inflation and rising interest rates have led to noticeable shifts in consumer spending and saving behaviors as Americans adapt to new economic realities. For many households, the immediate response to inflation is to prioritize essential spending over discretionary purchases. This shift is reflected in the changing patterns of consumer spending, with a greater portion of income being allocated to food, housing, and transportation, while spending on items like electronics, dining out, and travel may be reduced.

One significant behavioral change has been an increased focus on budgeting. As costs rise, consumers are more likely to track their expenses and actively seek ways to cut back. This might include buying in bulk, switching to generic brands, or shopping at discount stores. In some cases, households have also turned to lifestyle changes, such as cooking at home instead of eating out or opting for public transportation to save on fuel costs. These adjustments reflect a more cautious approach to spending, as people seek to stretch their dollars further in an inflationary environment.

Additionally, many Americans have re-evaluated their savings and debt management strategies. High inflation erodes the purchasing power of cash savings, leading some households to invest in assets that are more likely to appreciate over time, such as stocks, real estate, or even precious metals. However, the rising cost of living also means that many families have had to dip into their savings to cover expenses, resulting in a decline in the average household savings rate. At the same time, there is increased awareness of the importance of emergency savings, as economic uncertainty has underscored the need for financial resilience.

Another major shift has been in borrowing behavior. High inflation often coincides with higher interest rates, as the Federal Reserve raises rates to cool the economy. As a result, consumers are more cautious about taking on new debt, particularly for non-essential purchases. While demand for mortgages and auto loans may persist out of necessity, discretionary borrowing—such as for vacations or home renovations—has declined. For existing debt, many consumers are working to pay down balances more aggressively, recognizing that high interest rates make debt servicing more expensive.

The impact of inflation on financial behavior extends beyond individual households to the broader economy. As consumers spend more conservatively and focus on essentials, businesses in discretionary sectors may see reduced revenues, potentially leading to slower economic growth. In response, companies may adjust their pricing strategies or offer promotions to attract budget-conscious shoppers. These changes illustrate the complex interplay between inflation, consumer behavior, and economic activity.

In summary, high inflation has led to a more frugal mindset among consumers, with greater emphasis on budgeting, essential spending, and debt management. These behavioral shifts highlight the resilience of American households as they adapt to economic pressures. However, they also underscore the challenges that inflation poses to financial well-being, as consumers are forced to make difficult trade-offs to maintain stability.

The Inflation Effect demonstrates the far-reaching impact of rising prices on debt levels, income, and consumer behavior. Inflation not only increases the cost of borrowing and daily expenses but also reshapes financial priorities, prompting Americans to adjust their spending, saving, and borrowing habits in response to economic pressures. As the relationship between income growth and inflation continues to evolve, so too will the financial landscape for American households, emphasizing the need for proactive strategies to navigate the challenges of an inflationary economy.

Chapter 5:

Debt as a Tool - The Benefits and Risks of Leveraging Credit

Debt can be both a powerful tool for growth and a potential pitfall for households, depending on how it is used and managed. This chapter explores the dual nature of debt, focusing on its benefits when used as a means of financial empowerment, as well as the risks that arise when debt becomes unmanageable. By understanding how debt can support long-term financial goals, and recognizing the dangers of high-interest and excessive borrowing, households can make informed decisions about their financial strategies. Additionally, practical debt management approaches are outlined to help households maintain financial stability and resilience.

Positive Aspects of Household Debt

Debt, when managed well, can serve as a bridge to greater financial security and growth. This is especially true when debt enables investments in assets or resources that can increase in value over time or provide long-term benefits.

Investments in Housing, Education, and Vehicles

One of the most significant ways debt supports economic growth and personal wealth is through housing. Mortgage loans enable individuals and families to purchase homes that would otherwise be financially out of reach. Homeownership provides stability, allows households to build equity, and often serves as an appreciating asset over time. In many cases, the cost of a mortgage payment is comparable to, or even less than, the cost of renting a similar property. As a result, purchasing a home through debt can actually be a more cost-effective choice in the long run. Real estate investments, funded by mortgages, contribute not only to individual wealth-building but also to broader economic growth, as property ownership increases demand in construction, retail, and service sectors.

Education is another area where debt plays a critical role in personal development and economic productivity. Student loans allow individuals to pursue higher education or vocational training, which often leads to greater earning potential and career advancement. Studies consistently show that college graduates have higher average incomes than those with only a high school diploma, meaning that student debt, when it leads to a degree and employment, often pays off over time. Though student loans have risks, particularly if borrowers do not complete their degrees or secure high-paying jobs, they can still serve as a powerful investment in one's earning potential and skill set.

Similarly, auto loans allow individuals to purchase vehicles that are essential for work, school, and other activities that require reliable transportation. A car loan might enable someone to commute to a higher-paying job, pursue new employment opportunities, or access essential services. Although cars are depreciating assets, meaning they lose value over time, they provide critical functionality that can significantly affect an individual's quality of life and work prospects. For many households, the immediate benefits of owning a vehicle justify the cost of an auto loan, as it can open doors to higher earnings and greater convenience.

Credit as a Tool for Financial Empowerment
Credit availability empowers households to meet financial goals, manage emergencies, and even grow wealth, provided it is used responsibly. Access to credit, such as credit cards or personal loans, can help individuals bridge financial gaps during times of unexpected expenses or reduced income. For example, if a family encounters a medical

emergency or a home repair, having a credit line available allows them to cover these costs without liquidating assets or seeking alternative financing.

Credit can also be used as a tool for managing cash flow and even building credit history, which is essential for accessing better borrowing terms in the future. A positive credit history can lead to lower interest rates on mortgages, car loans, and personal loans, which means reduced costs over time. For those looking to establish or improve their credit, responsibly using credit cards — making small purchases and paying off balances monthly — can build a solid credit score without incurring significant interest.

Furthermore, debt can serve as an investment in small businesses or entrepreneurial ventures. Many successful businesses began with loans or credit lines that allowed owners to acquire inventory, pay for marketing, or cover startup costs. Though small business debt carries risks, it also represents an opportunity for wealth creation and independence.

Risks of Rising Debt Levels

While debt can be a valuable financial tool, it also carries risks, particularly when borrowing is excessive or high-interest. Over-leveraging, or taking on too much debt relative to one's income, can lead to financial instability and compromise an individual's ability to manage even small financial setbacks.

Financial Instability from Over-Leveraging

When households take on too much debt, they are at greater risk of financial hardship in the event of unexpected expenses or loss of income. Over-leveraging can make it difficult for individuals to meet monthly obligations, and it reduces the ability to save or invest for the future. During economic downturns, over-leveraged households are often hit hardest, as job loss or reduced income can quickly make debt repayments unaffordable. For instance, in the event of a recession, individuals with large mortgage, auto loan, and credit card payments may struggle to cover all their expenses, potentially leading to foreclosure, repossession, or bankruptcy.

In addition, high debt levels can create a financial dependency cycle, where individuals continue borrowing just to manage existing debt payments. This creates a "debt spiral," where the cumulative effect of interest payments and fees further increases total debt, making it increasingly challenging to escape.

The Dangers of High-Interest Debt

Not all types of debt are created equal; high-interest debt, particularly credit card debt, is one of the most financially burdensome. Credit cards often carry interest rates above 20%, meaning that even a relatively small balance can accrue significant interest charges if not paid off in full each month. High-interest debt can become unmanageable, as monthly payments primarily cover interest, with minimal impact on the principal balance. This type of debt can snowball over time, making it nearly impossible to pay off without drastic changes in spending or an influx of income.

Furthermore, high-interest debt can restrict households' financial flexibility, as a substantial portion of income may go toward servicing debt rather than saving or investing. For those who rely heavily on credit cards, the cost of purchases increases dramatically over time, reducing disposable income and potentially leading to a diminished quality of life. It's critical for households to carefully consider the interest rates of any debt they take on, as high-interest obligations can lead to long-term financial stress.

Debt Management Strategies for Households

Debt management strategies are essential for households aiming to use credit responsibly and avoid the pitfalls associated with high debt levels. By implementing practical approaches to managing and repaying debt, individuals can strengthen their financial health, reduce stress, and build long-term security.

Budgeting

A solid budget forms the foundation of effective debt management. Budgeting helps individuals understand their income, expenses, and discretionary spending, allowing them to make informed decisions about how to allocate funds. By tracking monthly income and categorizing expenses, households can identify areas where they may be overspending and reallocate funds toward debt repayment. For example, cutting back on non-essential purchases or subscriptions can free up extra money each month, which can then be applied to debt balances.

Budgeting also helps households plan for periodic expenses, such as insurance premiums or holiday gifts, reducing the likelihood of turning to credit to cover these costs. Creating a budget is an empowering tool that allows individuals to prioritize their financial goals, monitor their progress, and avoid unnecessary debt accumulation.

Building Emergency Savings

Emergency savings are critical for financial resilience, as they provide a safety net that can prevent households from going into debt when faced with unexpected expenses. While it may seem challenging to save while managing debt, even small contributions to an emergency fund can make a difference. A basic emergency fund of three to six months' worth of living expenses can help cover short-term income loss, medical bills, or urgent repairs, reducing reliance on credit cards or personal loans.

Setting aside a portion of each paycheck, even if it's only a small amount, can gradually build an emergency fund. Some individuals may choose to automate transfers to a separate savings account to ensure consistent contributions. While building an emergency fund takes time, it is an investment in financial stability that ultimately reduces debt dependency and stress.

Debt Repayment Plans

There are several effective strategies for paying down debt, and selecting the right approach depends on the types and amounts of debt held. Two popular repayment strategies are the debt snowball and debt avalanche methods.

Debt Snowball: This method involves paying off the smallest debt balances first, regardless of interest rates, while making minimum payments on larger debts. Once the smallest debt is paid off, the funds used for that debt are then applied to the next smallest debt. The advantage of the debt snowball is that it provides a psychological boost, as individuals experience a sense of accomplishment with each cleared balance, motivating them to continue the process.

Debt Avalanche: In contrast, the debt avalanche method focuses on paying off debts with the highest interest rates first. By tackling high-interest balances, individuals reduce the total amount of interest paid over time, potentially leading to faster debt elimination. While the debt avalanche method is often more cost-effective, it may take longer to see progress if high-interest debts also have high balances.

Both methods have benefits, and individuals should select the strategy that aligns best with their financial situation and motivations. Additionally, consolidating debt through a low-interest personal loan or balance transfer credit card may help simplify payments and reduce overall interest costs.

Debt, when used strategically, can be an asset, enabling households to invest in education, housing, vehicles, and other essentials that can enhance quality of life and contribute to long-term financial success. However, debt must be approached with caution. Over-leveraging and high-interest debt can undermine financial security, trapping households in a cycle of payments and interest accumulation. By implementing thoughtful debt management strategies, such as budgeting, building emergency savings, and utilizing repayment plans, households can leverage debt as a positive force, maintaining financial health while working toward future goals. In today's complex financial landscape, understanding the benefits and risks of debt is essential for building a stable, prosperous future.

Chapter 6:

The Future of Debt and Income in America - Trends and Predictions

As Americans continue to navigate an economy marked by rising debt levels, inflation, and evolving job markets, understanding the future interplay between debt and income becomes essential for policymakers, economists, and everyday citizens alike. The following sections forecast trends in debt and income, explore the role of government policy, and outline strategies for American households to build resilience against financial uncertainty.

Forecasting Debt and Income Growth

The U.S. economy is characterized by an interconnected relationship between debt and income, with inflation and interest rates acting as critical influences. To project where this relationship may head in the coming years, it's crucial to consider recent data alongside historical trends.

Debt Trends and Projections

As of the latest data, U.S. household debt has reached nearly $18 trillion, with credit cards, auto loans, and mortgages comprising significant portions. This trend has largely been fueled by increased consumer spending, inflation, and higher living costs. Analysts expect these factors to remain influential, with consumer debt likely continuing its upward trajectory in the near term. Mortgage debt, in particular, may see increased rates due to persistent home-price inflation and elevated demand, especially in urban areas.

In addition to rising home prices, auto loan debt has become a growing concern. Supply chain disruptions during the COVID-19 pandemic have driven up both new and used car prices, leading more consumers to finance vehicle purchases. This reliance on auto loans may increase further if car prices do not stabilize, exacerbating household debt burdens.

Credit card debt is also projected to increase as households grapple with higher costs in food, energy, and other essential goods. For lower-income households, rising credit card balances often lead to greater financial strain, particularly if interest rates continue to climb.

Income Growth Trends and Projections

On the income side, the U.S. economy has shown positive trends. Wage growth has consistently outpaced inflation over the past 18 months, buoyed by a strong labor market and low unemployment. However, income growth is expected to vary widely across industries, with technology, finance, and health care likely seeing stronger wage increases, while sectors such as retail and hospitality may experience slower growth.

Wage increases also depend on factors like technological advancement and labor market dynamics. The growth of remote work, for instance, has expanded job opportunities beyond regional constraints, allowing some workers to pursue higher-paying roles in major cities without relocating. However, automation and artificial intelligence may also lead to wage stagnation or job displacement in sectors where machines can replace routine work. Consequently, while income may continue to rise for many, disparities are likely to grow between high-skill and low-skill jobs, further impacting debt management capabilities across demographics.

Interest Rates and Inflation

The Federal Reserve's interest rate policy plays a central role in shaping both debt and income trends. Interest rates are projected to remain elevated in response to ongoing inflation concerns, though the Fed may slow rate hikes if inflationary pressures begin to ease. Higher interest rates typically mean higher costs for mortgages, credit cards, and loans, impacting household budgets and limiting disposable income.

Inflation is expected to remain above pre-pandemic levels, but may gradually decline if supply chain issues improve and global energy prices stabilize. However, any major economic shock—such as an oil price spike or another supply chain disruption—could trigger renewed inflationary pressures, complicating debt repayment and income stability for many households.

Policy Implications and Government Role

Given the economic pressures households face, government intervention can play a key role in managing debt and supporting income stability. Several policy options are available to help individuals manage debt, protect income, and encourage economic growth.

Interest Rate Adjustments

The Federal Reserve uses interest rate adjustments as a primary tool to control inflation and stabilize the economy. Raising interest rates helps curb excessive borrowing by making credit more expensive, which can reduce consumer spending and cool inflation. However, higher rates also make debt repayment more difficult, particularly for credit card holders and those with variable-rate loans.

Conversely, if inflation falls and economic growth slows, the Fed may lower interest rates to stimulate borrowing and spending. Lower rates make loans more affordable, potentially supporting income growth and reducing debt burdens. For the foreseeable future, it is likely that the Fed will maintain a cautious approach, adjusting rates as needed to balance inflation control with economic stability.

Student Loan Forgiveness and Reform

Student debt remains a significant financial burden for millions of Americans, impacting their ability to buy homes, start businesses, and contribute to the economy. Recent discussions around student loan forgiveness highlight the potential for policy reform in this area. Partial or full student loan forgiveness could free up income for many borrowers, reducing financial stress and potentially boosting consumer spending.

Beyond forgiveness, policymakers may explore reforms such as capping interest rates on student loans, expanding income-driven repayment options, and increasing funding for scholarships and grants. These measures could make higher education more affordable and reduce the likelihood of future debt accumulation among students.

Affordable Housing Initiatives

Rising housing costs contribute significantly to household debt, particularly in urban areas where home prices and rents have soared. The government can play a role in addressing housing affordability through incentives for affordable housing development, down-payment assistance programs for first-time homebuyers, and rent control measures in high-cost regions. Reducing housing costs can improve household budgets and allow families to allocate more income toward savings and debt repayment.

Financial Literacy Programs

Financial literacy remains a crucial but underemphasized area of policy intervention. Many Americans lack a solid understanding of basic financial principles, leading to costly mistakes in budgeting, debt management, and retirement planning. Governments, schools, and community organizations can expand financial education initiatives to equip individuals with the skills they need to manage debt, understand interest rates, and make informed investment decisions.

Tax Policies to Boost Disposable Income

Adjustments to tax policy could provide relief to households struggling with debt. For instance, expanding tax credits for low- and middle-income families, increasing the standard deduction, or implementing tax breaks on student loan interest could help families keep more of their income. Such measures would improve disposable income and reduce reliance on credit to meet daily expenses.

Building Financial Resilience for American Households

Financial resilience is the ability of households to withstand economic shocks and manage financial stress. Building resilience is increasingly important as economic uncertainty persists, and the following strategies can help individuals and families strengthen their financial positions.

Financial Literacy and Budgeting Skills

Developing financial literacy is foundational to managing debt and building wealth. Households benefit from understanding the basics of budgeting, interest rates, credit scores, and investment options. Financial literacy programs offered through schools, employers, and community centers can provide valuable insights into managing debt and preparing for unexpected expenses.

Budgeting, in particular, is an effective tool for maintaining financial control. By creating a budget, individuals can allocate funds for essential expenses, debt repayment, and savings, ensuring they are not overly reliant on credit. Modern budgeting tools and apps offer user-friendly ways to track spending, set goals, and monitor progress.

Emergency Savings

Establishing an emergency fund is critical for financial resilience. Emergency savings provide a safety net for unexpected expenses, such as medical bills, car repairs, or job loss. Financial experts generally recommend saving at least three to six months' worth of living expenses in a separate account.

Building an emergency fund may be challenging, especially for those with significant debt or low incomes. However, setting aside even a small amount regularly can accumulate over time, providing a cushion against financial setbacks and reducing the need to rely on high-interest debt in emergencies.

Investing in Income-Generating Skills

Education and skill development can be powerful tools for increasing income and financial resilience. In a rapidly changing job market, individuals benefit from continuous learning and skill-building. Acquiring in-demand skills, such as data analysis, coding, healthcare expertise, or project management, can open doors to higher-paying roles and greater career flexibility.

Online courses, certification programs, and trade schools offer affordable avenues for skill acquisition. For those looking to change careers or pursue advancement, investing in education can provide long-term financial benefits, reducing reliance on debt and improving future income prospects.

Strategic Debt Management

For those with significant debt, developing a strategic repayment plan is essential. Methods like the debt snowball (paying off the smallest debts first) and the debt avalanche (paying off the highest-interest debts first) can help borrowers manage and reduce their debt effectively. Consolidation options, such as refinancing student loans or using balance transfer credit cards, may also offer lower interest rates, reducing monthly payments and freeing up funds for savings.

Planning for Economic Shifts

Given the potential for economic volatility, households benefit from anticipating and preparing for changes in the economy. This may include diversifying income sources, such as taking on freelance work or investing in passive income streams, to reduce dependence on a single source of income.

Additionally, staying informed about economic trends, interest rates, and inflation can help individuals make informed financial decisions. For example, if interest rates are expected to rise, homeowners with adjustable-rate mortgages may consider refinancing to a fixed-rate loan to lock in a lower rate. Preparing for economic shifts enables households to remain resilient in the face of changing financial conditions.

In summary, the future of debt and income in America will likely continue to be shaped by complex economic factors, policy decisions, and individual financial choices. While rising debt levels and inflation pose challenges, opportunities exist for income growth and financial stability. By fostering financial literacy, encouraging proactive debt management, and supporting policies that alleviate financial stress, the U.S. can help households build resilience and secure a more stable financial future. For individuals and families, understanding and implementing these strategies will be essential to navigating the ever-evolving landscape of debt and income in America.

www.ingramcontent.com/pod-product-compliance
Lightning Source LLC
Chambersburg PA
CBHW070131230526
45472CB00004B/1504